REAL MEN DON'T COOK QUICHE

In true, Real Man fashion, this book offers food for thought.

Not to mention the fact that if you're ever stuck in France, it also offers a way to avoid starvation:

Take the book, place it in a 350-degree oven for 20 minutes and smother with ketchup.

Admittedly, a Real Man will not find this as satisfying as a cheeseburger.

But it's certainly more palatable than, say, quiche.

Published by New English Library:
REAL MEN DON'T EAT QUICHE
REAL MEN DON'T COOK QUICHE

REAL MEN DON'T COOK QUICHE

The Real Man's Cookbook

by Scott Redman
edited by Bruce Feirstein

additional True Brit material
by Lionel Trippett

Illustrated by Lee Lorenz
and David Austin

NEW ENGLISH LIBRARY

This essay is dedicated to David Redman,
A Real Man whose heart was as big
as his appetite.

All books are collaborative efforts. And since Real Men *do* give credit where
credit is due, the following people must be thanked for their contributions:
Marty Asher, Roger Bilheimer, Anne Maitland, Peter Minichiello, Trish Todd,
Nina Jorgensen, Darlene DeLillo, and Milton Charles from Pocket Books;
Jacques Chazaud; Lee Lorenz (whose drawings are as important as any word in
this essay); the Irv Schecter Company; the Ziegler Diskant talent agency; Nancy
Jean Gell; Tim Bernett; Steve Cass; Jake Bloom; Jonathan Roberts and, finally,
three people who made everything possible: Frank E. and Suzanne J. Schwartz,
and Jim Morgan, from *Playboy* magazine.

Scott Redman
Bruce Feirstein
September, 1982

First published in the USA in 1982 by Pocket Books, a Simon & Schuster division
of Gulf & Western Corporation.

First NEL Paperback edition May 1983

NEL Books are published by
New English Library,
Mill Road, Dunton Green,
Sevenoaks, Kent.
Editorial office: 47 Bedford Square, London WC1B 3DP

Typeset by Yale Press Ltd London SE25 5LY
Printed by Richard Clay (The Chaucer Press) Ltd, Bungay, Suffolk

0 450 05606 6

Contents

Introduction

Flex Crush was sitting at the Formica counter of Rosie's all-night diner in Tenafly, New Jersey. The restaurant smelled of bacon and fresh-brewed coffee. The fluorescent lighting glared. It was 5.30 a.m., and dawn was about to break over what passes for a horizon in the Garden State.

As Flex used a poppy-seed roll to wipe up the remains of a half dozen fried eggs from his plate – noting that Real Men do not believe in cholesterol – he made his final pronouncement on food.

'Real Men don't cook,' Flex sighed, 'they thaw.'

With this, the self-proclaimed Last Real Man in America stood, paid the check and walked out to drive his 18-wheel Kenworth onto the entrance ramp of the New Jersey State Turnpike, which many suspect is the final resting place of Jimmy Hoffa. Having consumed a full breakfast, Flex was ready to roll on another high-speed, cross-country, nuclear-waste delivery.

Yet as he pulled out of the parking lot, heading for the Vince Lombardi toll plaza, something he said struck us as odd.

Perhaps Flex – the divine arbiter of all things Real Man-ish, the great soothsayer and Kunta Kinte of American Real Men – well, perhaps Flex was wrong.

For while it is true that there may be better places for a man to distinguish himself than in the kitchen (including the Seville bull-ring, Barcelona's Nou Camp stadium, the Chicago Commodities exchange and centre ice at a Toronto Maple Leafs game), there is nevertheless no shame in his being able to find his way around a kitchen.

Especially if he's stuck in a logging camp during an avalanche, trying to woo Candice Bergen or just having friends over to break bread on the Real Man's high holy day – Superbowl Sunday – when no self-respecting Real Man restaurant owner would be open in the first place.

This book is designed to help men survive under these straits.

Because, after all, it only stands to reason that if a Real Man can put together the inter-state-highway system, surely he ought to be able to put together a decent meal for his buddies.

Introduction to the True Brit Edition

See the Introduction to the True Brit Edition of *Real Men Don't Eat Quiche*. Real Men (and particularly True Brit Real Men) don't need to be told the same thing twice. They either get the point first time round or they're not interested anyway.

Preface to the True Brit Edition

Q. When do True Brit Real Men cook?
A. When they have to.

For instance, as Real Man journeys through Life there comes a time between leaving home and getting married when he cannot always count on having a woman about the place to cook for him.

At this point the Quiche Eater learns to cook.

But Real Man does not give up so easily. He realises that what is needed is a series of temporary women to do the necessary. Real Man knows that this is not exploitation, rather he is granting a series of auditions to women who have to prove themselves worthy of wifedom some day.

However the logistics of making sure that there is always some handy woman on tap can prove pretty tricky at times. The experienced Real Man knows that an invitation to 'Come over to my place and I'll show you a Good Time in return for you doing supper, breakfast and cleaning out the kitchen' does not always work.

Stratagem number two is to try to get a blonde Swedish *au pair* called Ingrid installed on the premises. This has its obvious attractions but can lead to a diet of pickled herring, black rye bread and shredded cabbage. Also blonde Swedish *au pairs* called Ingrid tend to want a room of their own, six days off a week in order to perfect their English at the disco and the right to bring their own men home for the night. They are also over-frank (i.e. talkative) about matters gynaecological. No Real Man wants to have to listen to clinical details about Fallopian tubes over his bacon and eggs.

Strategem three is Eating Out. But this is expensive and can lead to inadvertent Quiche-exposure if you pick the wrong place. Also it can be inconvenient as Real Man often wants to eat in a hurry in the intervals between doing Real Things – like during the half-time adverts when the football is on TV, while waiting for the concrete mix to set or before going off to the pub.

And even when Real Man has got himself a proper live-in cook, there will be times when the plucky little woman is off sick and he has to cope. Then it is that he rises to the occasion and fends for himself. Then it is that Man the Hunter can be found reading *Sporting Life* behind a trolley full of lager and Vesta currys in the checkout queue at the supermarket. And then it is that Real Man discovers that no woman has a properly equipped kitchen. That is, after he has discovered where the kitchen is in the first place.

Fire's ok, but I still prefer to thaw it and eat it.

An Overview of Food

In the beginning, everything lived in the sea. It was cold. And dark. And a little too heavily salted for most people's taste.

Lo and behold, one day things began to change.

A certain group of fish decided to leave. They were hungry. And thirsty. And, realising that it was impossible to get a decent cup of coffee under water, they took to the land in search of a hot meal.

(Certain scientists have postulated this group of sea hunters were known as the 'Lloyd Bridges school of fish,' but this has yet to be scientifically proven.)*

Anyway, to make a long story short, this is how modern man came into being.

But we're not talking about Cro-Magnon man. Or Neanderthal man. No. The man we're talking about here is beef-eating man. A *Real Man* who would later invent the hamburger. And beer. And French fries. A Man who would reject such foolish notions as calories,

---

*On another note, it's theorised that a separate school of fish existed which found life too hectic in prehistoric urban society and chose to return to the sea. These spineless, gutless mammals are known today as dolphins and whales, and their wimpy traits may account for their current status as the darlings of the quiche-eating environmentalist crowd.

If you don't believe this, just consider the personalities of leading TV animal stars: Rin Tin Tin was a Real Man; ditto for Trigger, Mister Ed and Lassie. But Flipper? We strongly suspect he lives in Marina Del Rey, drives a Corvette and munches on quiche at every opportunity.

nutrition and vitamins – and would understand that a well-balanced diet consists of a quarter-pounder in each hand.

And so it came to pass that the ritual of eating was established.

Fire, for example, was discovered because Real Men had a primaeval instinct to barbecue.

The church immediately recognised the trend and incorporated the phrase 'thou preparest a table before me' in their service.

And this, of course, is without taking into account such important cultural milestones as the Last Supper, Jack Nicholson ordering a chicken-salad sandwich in *Five Easy Pieces* or the Earl of Sandwich inventing convenience foods.

But we digress.

The point is that food has always played an integral part in the Real Man's life. Food is the thing that fuels Real Men on the professional bowling tour. It's the primary source of nourishment for Mafia hit men, corporate lawyers, steelworkers, and auto-repossession experts. Food gives Men something to do at half time; it's a pleasant diversion at family gatherings (enabling you to avoid discussing religion with your aunts), and, of course, without food there would be no wonderful Real Man expressions like 'Eat my dust,' 'Bite the bullet,' 'I'm going to chew you up and spit you out,' and the ever-popular 'This ain't gonna be a piece of cake.'

In addition to all this, we must not overlook the fact that – perhaps most importantly –

eating is an essential part of the mating process.

First, because all Real Men know that a
good meal will always impress a date.

And, second, because it will give them the
strength and stamina to go the distance at the
end of the evening.

Real Men, you see, recognise that they
have more than one kind of insatiable appetite.

Real Man Cooking Lesson No 1

Five things that taste better with Jameson's
poured over them:
1. Shredded Wheat
2. Chicken
3. Ice
4. Salad
5. Anything served up to you on an aeroplane

Real Man Cooking Lesson No 2

Three things Real Men do not eat:
Crow
Their hearts out
Humble pie

An apple! I gave up a perfectly good rib for an apple?

The Kitchen: Real or Quiche?

First things first. How to locate the kitchen.

Most Real Men know where it is already. After all it's where most women spend much of their time and it is only prudent for a man to have some idea of what his wife is actually up to when she's out of his sight for a prolonged period of time.

It is also a place that has many more uses than just food preparation. For instance where better to strip down your Triumph Bonneville when the timing needs adjusting. The draining board was clearly invented with the home mechanic in mind. Where better to put all those fiddly bits that would otherwise just roll under the sofa. The sink is an ingenious device. Not only can you use it for cleaning tar, heavy-duty oil and earth from under the finger nails, but it is also, as mentioned in a previous book*, a useful place when you're caught short. The refrigerator has long been discovered by Real Man as the perfect place to keep such necessities as 35mm film, small batteries, beer and Superglue.

Incidentally a kitchen has a further use. It adds considerably to the resale value of a house. It should not therefore be removed or turned into a recording studio or two-bay inspection pit.

*Real Men Don't Each Quiche, p.76

If however you're still not sure where it is, it's probably where you eat breakfast and the place where most other meals come from. Any last lingering doubt is best dealt with by bringing a woman into the house. Any woman will do. She'll instinctively head for the kitchen like a rat going for a drainpipe.

The Real Kitchen

Should contain:

Several frying pans – at least enough to avoid washing up for a week.

Tin openers – a complete range. Make sure that at least one is of the old stab-and-hack variety with no moving parts to go wrong.

Knives – steak knives, meat cleavers, boning knives etc – all razor sharp. Real Men use knives for all forms of food preparation: levering the lids off tins of custard powder, slashing open packets, prizing fried eggs off the bottom of the pan and puncturing party-size beer cans.

Knife sharpeners – to include a steel, an oilstone and a backdoor step. Ideally a Real Man would like a steam-driven knife grinder so that he could watch the in-and-out thrust of giant pistons while the toast burns.

Saucepans – these should be very large, sufficient for a four-day, reheated, all-in stew.

Remember to boil all vegetables for at least an hour. No Real Man eats them raw. The ultimate Quiche expression is *al dente*. This means still hard in Real language.

A cooker – gas not electric. Real Men like to see the flames when they're cooking. They recognise only two gas settings: Full On and Off and don't mess with anything in between. Real Men prefer to cook on top of the stove so that they can keep an eye on what is going on and put it out in order to prevent the arrival of three fire engines, all loaded to the gills with other Real Men intent on axeing down the front door and blasting the entire place apart with high-pressure hoses. Real Men have a great respect for the Fire Brigade and know that, on form, they can create more havoc in ten minutes than Goering's Luftwaffe managed during the entire London blitz.

Storage space – for bulk emergency supplies of boil-in-the-bag instant meals. Other food comes in tins – preferably the giant caterers' sizes.

The Quiche Kitchen

Equally important is what you won't find in a Real Man's kitchen. There will be no ceramic hobs, digital clock read-outs built in to the oven, no *en suite* working surfaces or eye-level grills, no plumbed-in waste disposal units in the sink. (Actually, Real Men think the best use ever made of a waste disposal unit came in the film *Rolling Thunder* when William Devane had his hand shoved down one. The *Time Out*/NFT school of film criticism would no doubt defend this as some kind of meaningful psycho-sociological metaphor. Real Men simply accept it as a piece of gratuitous violence and sensationalism. And loved every minute of it. Apart from this, waste disposal units are responsible for more bent teaspoons than Uri Geller ever managed.)

Nor will a Real Man have any truck with woks, Slo-cookers, Tandoori ovens, Magi-Mixes or Robochefs. In short Real Man will not tolerate a kitchen that looks like a cross between a 747 flight deck and the control room at Three Mile Island. Because Real Men know that cooking is simple.

It is also a work place, pure and simple. He leaves it to the Quiche Eater to decorate and prettify the kitchen with twee, heart-shaped magnets on the fridge door, striped aprons, cat calenders, bunches of clipped recipes in a giant paper clip and National Trust drying-up cloths with pictures of cottage gardens. Real Men don't in general dry up but they'll occasionally wipe a dirty fork or lipsticked glass on their sweaters at the last moment.

Where the Quiche Eater has a spice rack, Real Man has a brown sauce rack.

An Interview With the Ultimate Real Man Chef

The problem was obvious.

Having firmly established that Real Men don't eat quiche, millions of people (thousands, anyway) have hungered after a simple answer:

Just what *do* Real Men eat?

What are the foodstuffs that satiate them when there's no McDonald's, Kentucky Fried Chicken or Little Chefs within excessive speeding distance?

Thirsting after this knowledge, we decided to visit the world's foremost expert in Real Men's cuisine, Rocco (the Knife) Tortellini, current head chef at Joliet State Prison.

As we began the interview, Rocco was putting the finishing touches on a luncheon for 1,200 close friends and former business associates.

Q. What are you serving today?
A. Twelve to fifteen for grand theft, conspiracy and extortion, reducible to six weeks for good behaviour.
Q. No. We meant for lunch.
A. Oh. It's something called prison stew. The recipe is 1,200 pounds of beef, plus 400 pounds of potatoes and a handful of vege-

tables. You cut it all up, throw it in a pot and let it simmer until parole.

Q. Does anybody complain about the food?

A. Not if they're smart.

Q. What do you think of the state of Real Men's cuisine today?

A. It makes me sick. In the old days, Real Men ate canned foods – and the can. They ate frozen foods frozen. They ate beef. Steak. Hamburgers, cheeseburgers, chilli burgers, bacon burgers, pizza burgers and ribs. Anything they could kill with a gun or grill.* But today things are different. You got guys in here who want stuff like Brie. Perrier. Cold pasta salad. Poached salmon in dill. I can understand poaching diamonds. But salmon? Next thing, they'll probably want finger bowls on the tables. If they'd served that stuff in the old days, you woulda had guys breakin' out not for freedom, but a decent meal.

Q. Why do you think this has happened?

A. I suppose it has something to do with the element crime is attracting today. When I first started you had thugs, button men, and racketeers. But now you've got guys in here for computer crime. Insurance fraud. Pansy stuff. I think the change started in the early '70s when we had all those guys from Watergate passing through. One of

*Actually, grilling was always the Real Man's favourite way to cook. After a tough day with the DA, it was nice to be on the other side of the table for a change.

them sent back a piece of meat that was too tough. Now that's a wimp for you. In the old days, a Real Man prided himself on being able to chew through cement.

As Rocco continued preparing lunch, the inmates poured into the dining room. He was correct that times had changed; instead of being filled with 'hard guys' like George Raft, Jimmy Cagney or Burt Lancaster (as the bird-man of Alcatraz), the joint was rotten with cocaine dealers, income tax evaders and Billie Sol Estes-type financial swindlers. It looked more like teatime in the IBM corporate dining room than chowtime at the Rock.

Glancing over the crowd, Rocco shrugged and continued cooking.

Q. Getting back to food, what are the basic eating habits of Real Men?
A. Real Men eat standing up. They eat with their friends. They eat with gusto. They also eat with veterans of foreign wars, cut-throat corporate executives and union officials.
Q. Is there anyone a Real Man won't eat with?
A. Hair stylists, distant cousins, interior decorators and anybody celebrating victory at a backgammon tournament.
Q. What's the main reason Real Men eat?
A. It cuts down on small talk.
Q. What about foreign food? Do Real Men eat guacamole? French food? Mexican food?
A. What do *you* think?

Q. Well, if you were stuck in a foreign country, there's a chance you might have to –
A. Wrong. When a Real Man gets hungry
overseas, he eats K rations. Or he stops in
the cafeteria of the American embassy and
gets a real meal.
Q. Do Real Men always finish what's on their
plates?
A. Yeah. But only because they're hungry.
Never because children are starving in
places like India, Europe, French res-
taurants or the Republic of Togo.
Q. Do you have any tips for Real Men chefs
who might be reading this book?
A. Yeah. Always make sure your oven is hot
enough to melt a Chevrolet.
Q. What about condiments?
A. I'm Catholic. I don't believe in birth control.

At this point, the interview was suddenly
cut short; inside the dining room the inmates
were pounding the table for dinner – and it
was Rocco's duty to answer their chant of,
'Granola, Granola, Granola.'

Unfortunately, this was to be his last duty
as chef.

In Rocco's own words, he'd 'cooked his
own goose' by serving one Real Man meal too
many – and was savagely brutalised with cold
pasta by several dozen irate inmates who were
serving time for 'grave offences in bad taste'
committed against the editors of *Architectural
Digest*.

Yet Rocco will not be forgotten.

Many of his recipes are reproduced in this book; in the end, he died so that you can eat better.

Real Man Cooking Quiz No 1

Q. Where does a Real Man eat in San Francisco?
A. Oakland.

Real Man Cooking Quiz No 2

Q. When do Real Men eat out?
A. When the wife's gone home to mother.

It happens every time the cook puts too much rosemary in the Veal Marengo.

Breakfast

Let's face it:

The Royal Engineers do not go to work on a belly filled with crepes.

And neither should you.

Yes, it's an undeniable fact that a Real Man needs a Real Breakfast in the morning.

And it doesn't matter whether you're a City stockbroker who's about to be indicted for inside trading or the member of the Royal Engineers who's responsible for wiping out the Natterjack toad because the simple truth is that *every* Real Man needs a hearty breakfast – not only to build up his stamina for the day ahead, but also help him recover from his sexual acrobatics the night before.

With this in mind, it should be obvious that Real Men do not begin their day with warm milk.

Real Men do not eat brunch.

They do not eat coddled eggs.

And they certainly don't start off the day with croissants, Ready-Brek, peach yoghurt or any kind of children's breakfast cereal that has pictures of cartoon characters on the box.

(Real Men understand that anyone who begins the day staring at a box of Ricicles or Cocoa Poufs will hardly be in the right frame of mind to stare down a hostile board of directors in the corporate conference room.)

So what *do* Real Men eat in the morning?

They eat poached eggs on Marmited toast or bubble and squeak, kippers or smoked haddock. They eat immense fry-ups of eggs, streaky bacon, sausages, black pudding, tomatoes, baked beans and fried bread. They mop up the grease with slice after slice of white bread. They tackle stacks of toast and thick-cut marmalade.

Real Men, you see, know that Major Sir Ranulph Twisleton-Wykeham-Fiennes did not go round the world from top to bottom by eating a breakfast of grapefruit and cottage cheese.

But if you're still uncertain about what to eat in the morning, the following may help: if a particular breakfast dish seems as though it might be best suited to people like David Frost, Russell Grant or David Owen, pass it by immediately.

But if on the other hand the food seems like something Jocky Wilson, Ian Botham, James Bolam, Ray Reardon, Daley Thompson or Albert Tatlock might enjoy, then it's odds on that you're on the right track.

Perfect Scrambled Eggs

Every Real Man loves eggs for breakfast — because it requires breaking them in the process of cooking.

(Put in more psychological terms, what could be better for a Real Man's spirit at 6 o'clock in the morning than the notion that he can beat mother nature?)

INGREDIENTS
3 large eggs
butter
tonic water*

To begin, break the eggs into a large bowl and beat them until thoroughly mixed.

(If you ordinarily avoid this kind of manual labour, don't worry; merely view it as therapeutic exercise and pretend the eggs represent VAT, DHSS or TV licence inspectors.)

Next, melt several tablespoons of butter into a large frying pan over a medium flame.

When the butter begins to smoke, add a shot of tonic to the egg mixture.

Then pour the mix into the frying pan, before the butter burns, and cook to taste.

The Morning-After Omelette

As we all know, everyone wakes up famished.

But as we also know, there's nothing more clichéd than offering to buy your date breakfast.

Thus, the morning-after omelette.

*The tonic makes the eggs lighter and fluffier. For an interesting variation, you can substitute champagne left over from the night before.

A perfect way to show a woman you're well rounded — and can exhibit the same prowess in the kitchen that you exhibited in the bedroom the night before.

INGREDIENTS
8 extra-large eggs
1 large green pepper
1 large onion
1lb cooked ham
½lb cheddar cheese
½lb Gruyère cheese
1 large tomato

First, chop the pepper, onion, tomato and ham into small pieces. (Red peppers, salami, mushrooms or anything else that seems vaguely edible in your refrigerator may be substituted.)

Second, beat the eggs in a bowl and add in all the chopped ingredients except for the cheese.

Next, melt several tablespoons of butter in a frying pan over a medium flame . . . And when the butter begins to smoke, pour the entire mixture into the pan.

When the concoction is half cooked, place the cheeses on top of the omelette and cover the entire frying pan with a pot lid.

Cook for a minute or two until the cheese melts, then add seasoning to taste.

Yield: 3 servings.

NOTE: Among the congnoscenti, this is

known as a garbage omelette, because it will not only impress your date but also use up any excess food in your refrigerator before it becomes mouldy and begins to look like a failed chemistry experiment.

Feel free to experiment and substitute things like leftover spaghetti sauce for cheese or, for the meat, try using the steak or lobster your date brought home from the restaurant in a doggie bag the night before.

Beyond this, in order to ensure the perfect romantic breakfast, just add hot buttered toast and thick-cut chunky marmalade, orange juice, any champagne left over from the night before – and the Sunday morning papers. (Especially if it's Saturday morning. She'll be amazed at your resourcefulness.)

Do remember one thing, however: no woman is impressed by last night's cold take-away pizza served in the cardboard container.

Ham Steak and Redeye Gravy

Imagine you're in Bismarck, North Dakota. It's dawn. The dead of winter. The snow is so high you can barely see over the basketball net in your driveway; the temperature is 50 degrees below zero. Inside the house.

This is the time for ham steak and redeye gravy.

You don't live in Bismarck, North Dakota?
It doesn't matter.
Because even if you reside in such quiche-

eating locales as Palm Springs, Palm Beach, or Wilton, Connecticut, one thing always remains the same:

In the cold, cruel, dog-eat-dog world of Real Men, *every* morning is 6 o'clock in the morning in the middle of December in Bismarck, North Dakota.

INGREDIENTS
1lb ham steak
black coffee

Start by cooking the ham steak slowly in a large skillet until tender – about 15 minutes.

Once this is finished, remove the ham and add 1½ cups of water to the skillet.

Bring the water to a boil and scrape all the cooking particles and red meat from the bottom of the pan; boil for several more minutes (until the mixture begins to thicken) and add several tablespoons of black coffee to darken and add taste to the gravy.

Serve with scrambled eggs and home fries – liberally pouring the gravy on the fries and ham steak.

Yield: 2 servings

Old-Fashioned Buttermilk Pancakes

Aunt Jemima's may be good, but these are better.

INGREDIENTS
4 large eggs
2½ pints buttermilk
1lb flour
2½ tsp baking powder
1 tsp salt
4oz melted butter

Beat the eggs in a bowl and add the buttermilk.

Mix, then pour the dry ingredients into the batter while stirring constantly. Continue stirring until the batter is smooth. If the batter is too thick to pour, add water.

Next, add the melted butter to the batter.

Heat a frying pan on a medium flame and prime with a tablespoon of butter.

Once the butter is bubbling, add the batter half a cup at a time to make man-sized flapjacks.

As soon as bubbles begin to appear on the surface of the batter, flip the pancake once.

Yield: 20 pancakes – enough for two members of any Alabama road gang.

NOTE: Use only pure maple syrup – the kind preferred by lumberjacks everywhere.

Mining Camp Potatoes

Every man needs a shot of starch in the morning.

And not just in his shirts.

INGREDIENTS
1¼lbs unsmoked back bacon, diced
6 potatoes, cut into man-sized chunks
1 large onion, chopped beyond recognition
1½ tsp salt
¼ tsp pepper

In a large skillet, cook the bacon until crisp.

Remove the bacon from the pan, but do not drain the fat.

Put the remaining ingredients into the bacon fat and toss them for two minutes over a high flame.

Return the cooked bacon to the skillet and *slowly* add warm water until the potatoes are three-quarters covered.

Finally, cover the pan and cook over a medium flame for twenty minutes.

(Admittedly, this is not as fast as McDonald's. But if it took twenty million years to create a masterpiece like the Grand Canyon, surely you can wait twenty minutes for great spuds.)

Yield: 4 servings

Rocky Mountain Toast

For years, people who've watched television
have had a simple set of questions:

What did Tonto feed the Lone Ranger?
What did Butch feed Sundance?
What did Cheyenne feed Sugarfoot?
What did Johnny feed the Rifleman?
What did Chester feed Matt Dillon?
What did Ben feed Hoss?

And – most importantly – what did The
Man With No Name feed himself – and his
mule?

To be honest, we don't know.

But we strongly suspect that if these brave,
upstanding men had started their day with
Rocky Mountain Toast, they would have lived
to die in gun battles, instead of getting killed in
the ratings.

INGREDIENTS
3 pieces soda bread
4 eggs
1oz butter
2 thick slices Canadian bacon or salami

Melt two tablespoons of butter in a skillet.

Take one slice of the bacon and sauté it over
a low flame until brown. (Note: For those of
you not intimately familiar with the cuisine of
our friends to the north, Canadian bacon looks
like a salami. And try not to remember that
this is the country that gave us a quiche-eater

like Pierre Trudeau – because it also gave us the National Hockey League.)

Now that you've finished musing about international politics, remove the bacon from the skillet and set it aside on a paper towel.

Next, take a piece of soda bread. Take a water glass, turn it upside down and punch a hole in the centre of the bread.

(Don't get carried away here and use such alternatives as a drill press, 12-gauge shotgun or – perish the thought – chain saw.)

To continue, place the bread in the skillet and brown it in the bacon fat and butter.

Once the bread is browned on one side, flip it over. (If the skillet is dry, add another tablespoon of butter.)

Let the other side of the bread brown for a minute. Once this is finished, crack an egg and place it in the centre of the bread – as if you were making a sunny-side-up egg.

As soon as the egg firms up, place the bacon on top.

Quickly flip the toast over to momentarily reheat the bacon, and serve.

Yield: 2 servings

Real Men sit down to eat.
Quiche Eaters stand up and nibble.

Congress House Doughnuts

Respectfully Dedicated
to Red Robbo, the Mole
and King Arthur

Taste these and you'll understand why the
unions have always negotiated for longer tea
breaks.

INGREDIENTS
1oz dried yeast
6 tbsp warm water + 1 tsp brown sugar
½ pint lukewarm milk
2 cups flour

   Start by dissolving the yeast in the water in
a large bowl. Once the yeast is *completely*
dissolved, add the remaining ingredients.
   Cover the bowl with a towel and place it in
a warm, draught-free area. Let the mixture rise
for 45 minutes.
   (A warm, draught-free area is the top of
your stove – *not* Brighton Conference Centre.)
   Now, take the following and with your
hands mix into another large bowl:

2½lbs flour
½lb sugar

1 tsp salt
¾lb softened butter
6 eggs
2 tbsp milk

After these ingredients are fully mixed, slowly add 1 pint of warm milk, mixing constantly until you have a soft dough.

Stir in the yeast mixture and knead the dough for several minutes.

Just to pass the time, here's a joke you may tell while you're doing this:

Question: What does a Real Man play on the piano?

Answer: Poker.

With the entertainment segment of the recipe completed, on a lightly floured board, roll the dough into cylinders four inches long and three-quarters of an inch wide.

Bring the ends of the cylinders together to form the doughnuts.

Next (and finally) lay the doughnuts out on a baking tray and let them rise until they are double their size.

With this completed, *fill* a *deep* pan with cooking oil, leaving 2 inches of room at the top, and heat to 375 degrees.

With a spatula, gently slide the doughnuts in and cook until golden brown.

Yield: 3 dozen

Bring Me the Plate of
Alfredo Garcia Sausage

If there is truly a Real Man's grande cuisine, this is it. What caviar is to lesser mortals, this is to Real Men.

It may take longer to prepare – but, like World War II, it's worth the struggle.

Before you start this recipe, go to a butcher and have him grind one pound of pork fat and two pounds of fresh lean pork meat together. Ham, loin or shoulder will suffice.

(You can do this at home if you have a meat grinder, paper shredder, or – heaven forgive us – if your wife owns a MagiMix.)

Next, prepare the following Alfredo Garcia sausage spice:

1 tbsp crushed bay leaves
1 tbsp ground cloves
1 tbsp mace (the spice, not the riot deterrent)
1 tbsp nutmeg
1 tbsp paprika
1 tbsp thyme
1½ tsp basil
1½ tsp cinnamon
1½ tsp oregano
1½ tsp sage
1½ tsp savory
2oz white peppercorns

Grind all these ingredients together – using a coffee mill, MagiMix, blender or spice mill.

Take two teaspoons of Al's spice (Real Men

can call each other by their nicknames), add one tablespoon of salt and beat it into the ground meat.

(With all the grinding and beating, it's no wonder this is named after Alfredo Garcia.)

Now cover the mixture and place it in the refrigerator for a minimum of 12 hours.

(In the interim defend the Alamo, or just teach someone a lesson.)

Welcome back.

Now the serious cooking begins.

Cover the bottom of a frying pan with a half inch of water.

Form the sausage mixture into small patties and cook over a low flame for 10 minutes or more, until cooked through.

IMPORTANT NOTE: Make *sure* the patties are cooked all the way through. Real Men can think of better things to die of than trichinosis.

Yield: 16 patties

Real Man Cooking Quiz No 3

Q. What's red and white and finely chopped?
A. Robert Carrier in a MagiMix.

Real Man Cooking Lesson No 3

Q. What does a Real Man use a wok for?
A. Oil Changes.

Interviews with True Brit Real Cooks (1)

If any place can be described as the shrine of True Brit Real Food, surely it must be the Transport Cafe. If any group can be described as summing up all that is Real in this great country of ours, surely it must be the long distance truck drivers. Stars of a thousand tele-commercials, their hairy tattooed fore-arms, string vests and plaid working shirts are enlarged to superhuman proportions as they loom above us on a million advertising hoard-ings. The open road ever before them, lords of all they survey, rescuers of hitchhiking dam-sels in distress, their coded headlight signals never quite understood by the envious private motorist, they are Real Men. And what they eat must be Real Food.

So, shaken by the tide of creeping Quichery that is engulfing the country, we set out on a pilgrimage of reaffirmation, heading for the one place where traditional Real Food Values must still reign supreme. We were not going to see the Lions of Longleat or the Typhoo chimps at teatime. We were off to see the truck drivers at breakfast. We knew what to expect: huge plates of egg, beans and chips, greasy bacon, piles of proper white bread and pint mugs of sweet tea.

Somewhere north of Stamford we found what we were looking for – a traditional roadside cafe surrounded by the traditional acres of hard core and oily puddles. We pulled in, noticed with approval the traditionally totally steamed-up windows and went in.

To be met by a surprise.

'I blame it all on the foreign trucks,' said Len, the owner. 'Foreign trucks, foreign habits and foreign food. One thing following the other as sure as night follows day. We began to notice the change soon after the big Volvos, Mercs and DAFs started to appear. I mean who'd call a truck a DAF, for God's Sake! First thing the demand for meat pies dropped. Remember the traditional meat pie? The ones where you'd cut 'em open and there'd be this big space inside. With something grey and lumpy crouching at the bottom like an alien life form that had slithered out of a UFO and crept inside to hide?

'Used to sell 'em by the hundred. But not any more. Then we found we were selling less beans . . . .'

We remembered those beans. How they came glued together in a clump that hit the bottom of the stomach like a lead ingot. How they stood up proudly on the plate like an island amid the swilling tide of lukewarm grease. How their remains stuck like Araldite between the prongs of the fork and defied the best efforts of any washing-up method known to man.

We fell silent, heads bowed in thought. And in the hush we heard the soft hiss of air brakes as a Magrus-Deutz with air-conditioned cab, power steering and TIR plates drew up outside.

'You'll see what I mean now,' said Len.

The driver, slim in his quilted nylon bomber jacket, designer jeans and training shoes, jumped down, came in and ordered.

'Slice of Quiche, Waldorf salad with chicory and small Lo-Cal Perrier water please,' and he retired to sit down out of earshot with his pocket calculator and his time sheets.

'Not how it used to be, is it? Where are the Seddons and ERGs of yesteryear? Where are the chassis delivery drivers with no cabs and seven layers of overcoat. Men with sump oil engrained in every pore. Fill one of 'em up with half a bottle of whisky, winch him up into the driver's seat and set him off. Go two hundred miles without so much as a piss-stop, pull in, fall off, frozen stiff, come to and eat three breakfasts on the trot . . . .'

We were interrupted by the squeal of brakes and a hideous crash. We ran outside. A bulk yoghurt tanker had skidded and overturned. A tidal wave of DairiFresh, Balkanstyle, low-fat natural yoghurt swept across the carriageway. Behind, the driver of a Scania loaded with bagged muesli fought the wheel as his truck aquaplaned across the central reservation, shedding rolled oats, bran, dried fruit and chopped nuts over three lanes. It was the man behind him who was in real trouble. His load shifted as he emergency braked. Twenty tons of Yorkie bars crashed through the back of the cab, burying him completely.

Plunging through the sucking morass of health food, we tore at the milk chocolate, raisin and biscuit mixture with our bare hands. It seemed impossible for anyone still to be alive underneath. Then Len pulled back. 'Listen,' he said. We listened. Faintly we could hear the cries of a human being in pain. 'The poor sod must be in agony,' said Len, 'but still alive.'

By now the yoghurt had seeped into the fractured Yorkie bars, turning them into a hellish sludge. 'I reckon we've got about ten minutes before this lot sets solid,' said Len. Frantically we probed the mix. The sounds of pain were louder now. Louder.

Instinctively we both stopped and turned to each other. An awful suspicion was hardening into appalling certainty. 'That noise,' I shuddered, 'I've heard it before.' 'Me too,' said Len, his eyes widening with horror. Grimly we dug on. Words were becoming distinct: *'Oh Mandy . . .'* 'It can't be,' said Len. ' *. . . you came and you gave . . .'* 'It is.' ' *. . . without taking . . . .'* 'Barry Manilow!'

Barry Manilow, coming through loud and clear on the in-cab stereo cassette deck, singing in the pain as a choking cloud of rye flakes stung and reddened our eyes.

Now we dug like men possessed, hoping against hope, shutting our ears to the terrible sound. And so we came to him. The driver. Peanuts and jagged splinters of crisp biscuit were embedded in his flesh. Tenderly we wiped the cocoa solids and vegetable fat from his face. The yoghurt froth round his lips showed that he was still breathing. Carefully, carefully, as Barry Manilow sang unstoppably on, we lifted him out, carried him into the cafe and laid him on the counter.

'Emergency fry-up,' said Len, pulling a two-pound package of lard from the First Aid kit by the tea urn. And he set to work; a Real Man doing a Real Man's job. Minutes later the driver opened his eyes. 'What . . . what happened . . . ? Where am I . . . ?' he murmured. 'Shhh, just lie still and eat this,' said Len, lifting a plate of two fried eggs, sausage and chips to his battered lips. 'You're going to be all right . . . .'

Our eyes met and an unspoken message passed between us. Real Man's food had saved the day.

Later Len and I agreed that there was no need for a special recipe, spelled out line by line. Any True Brit Real Man knows by instinct how to put together a proper high-cholesterol breakfast. So for all those doggedly ploughing their way through this book we suggest you take a natural break, harden your arteries and read on.

Any man who has dined on baked beans and five pints of Bass knows what it is to stand alone.

Lunch

It's midday.

You've topped out a 70-storey skyscraper, moved an 18-wheeler 1,000 miles, engineered the unfriendly takeover of a Fortune 500 company and loaded enough boxcars to stretch from here to Shreveport and back again.

No, this is not time for Miller.

It's time for lunch.

And contrary to the rantings and ravings of Congress, we're not talking about a simple dignified Blimpie Tuna on White Number 2.

No way.

The subject under discussion here is the fabulous three-martini, all-expenses-paid, slush-fund, American Express, IRS, expense-account extravaganza. The kind of meal that starts at noon and runs till 4.30; the kind of eating binge that keeps eminent cardiologists in business; the kind of lunch that manipulates stock prices, fixes union problems or puts you in partnership with John de Lorean.

So why, you may ask, is Congress so upset with the three-martini lunch?

It could be they prefer to start drinking before noon.

It started as a friendly disagreement over hockey
players, but then they started comparing chilli recipes,
and things got nasty.

Or it may just be another example of our government's colossal misunderstanding of the way American business works.*

Either way, however, we feel it's time that somebody set the world straight about this meal.

The American business lunch is the perfect time to exert undue influence on a union shop steward, set up a merger that will drive the Securities and Exchange Commission wild or just to look for another job.

It is *not* the time for white wine, fruit compote, poached salmon in a light dill sauce or a waiter who approaches your table by saying, 'Hi. My name is David, and I'll be serving you today.' (To this, Real Men always reply, 'Hi. My name is Vic, and I'll be leaving you now.')

Real Men, you see, understand there is no such thing as a free lunch – but they have absolutely no compunction about letting Uncle Sam underwrite a large portion of it.

This is not to say, however, that everyone has exactly the same perspective on this meal.

When Armand Hammer (chairman of the board of Occidental Petroleum) says he's going

---

*In the early 1800s, the French writer Alexis de Tocqueville was the first to point out that second-raters tend to run for political office in America – while the best and the brightest are attracted to the risks, rewards and challenges of commerce. De Tocqueville came to this conclusion after meeting various American politicians over lunch and dinner – all of which he is reputed to have 'put in' for. Had de Tocqueville been alive today, we're reasonably certain he would have postulated that Real Men create their own destiny – while Congressmen seem to do nothing but muck everyone else's up.

out for a business lunch, it usually means he's going to swallow an entire industry.

Harry Truman 'chewed out' Douglas Mac-Arthur.

And when Anthony 'Tony Pro' Provenzano talks about 'talkin' turkey,' other people get indigestion.

But no matter what, there is one simple, fundamental truth about the Real Man's lunch.

At noon, a Real Man needs a meal with legs on it. He needs something that will stick to his ribs, not merely to the roof of his mouth.

And whether it's delivered in a lunch pail, off the back of a canteen truck, or on a silver platter at the 21 Club, one thing is certain:

The day is yet young, and a Real Man needs nourishment.

Because there are still breeder reactors to fix, law-suits to file, Chevys to call back and lots of important police work ahead.

The Battle of Atlanta Fried Chicken

If nothing else, the Civil War was, well, civil.

They always broke for lunch. And, more often than not, they ate fried chicken.

The following recipe uses a peach sauce that was originated in the grand hotels of Atlanta. The dish is spicier than most of the frozen commercial varieties we've grown used

Well, well – a three martini lunch, Joey Martini, Al
Martini, and Nick, 'The Pliers,' Martini.

to, but if anyone complains, just say, 'Frankly, my dear, I don't give a damn.'

Especially if it's a man.

INGREDIENTS
2 cut-up chickens
1 pint milk
1 tsp Tabasco sauce
1lb flour
1½ tsp salt
2 chilli peppers, chopped fine
½ gallon of corn oil
A deep frying pan
One unsoiled brown grocery bag

To start, mix the milk and Tabasco sauce in a large bowl. Place the chicken parts into the bowl and refrigerate for at least one hour.

(If you don't have a watch, four innings of a baseball game, one period of hockey or one short phone call to your mother should suffice.)

Next, put the flour, salt and red pepper into the grocery bag. Clutch the bag at the top and shake to combine the ingredients.

Next, fill the frying pan with oil until it comes within one and a half inches of the top. Heat the oil over a medium flame until it just barely smokes.

At this point, remove the chicken from the refrigerator and drop it into the bag one piece at a time.

Shake the bag to make sure the chicken is completely coated.

Gently place the chicken in the oil, making sure not to splatter yourself.

Fry until golden brown – and cooked inside, about 8 to 10 minutes. During the cooking process, regulate the flame to make sure the chicken does not burn.

Serve smothered with the following Georgia peach sauce:

GEORGIA PEACH SAUCE INGREDIENTS
1 8oz jar of peach jam
4 tbsp of water
1 medium onion, sliced
4 tbsp butter
½ tsp paprika
juice of one lemon
1 tbsp white vinegar
1 tbsp brown sugar
½ tsp Worcester sauce

Combine all the ingredients in a saucepan and bring to a boil.

Turn down the heat and simmer (partially covered) for 10 minutes.

Once you've tasted this, you too will wonder how the South lost.

Yield: 6 servings

Hamburger

Alas, the quiching of America has reached the hamburger.

Unfortunately, it seems that every two-bit

salad-and-yoghurt joint in the country has found it necessary to come up with a different name for this dish.

And with things like Alpine burgers, Rancho burgers, Big Macs, Whoppers, Grand Wizard of the KKK burgers and Salisbury steak, can Quiche burgers be far behind?

By the Real Man's way of thinking, this is, well, stupid.

A hamburger is a hamburger. And there's only one acceptable variation: the bacon cheeseburger.

They're America's holy food, and no World Series, poker game, or first teenage date would be complete without them. (In fact, it's even been suggested that Uncle Sam should pass them out to democratic converts the way the Pope hands out holy wafers.)

Now, admittedly, the following recipe may be more interesting and tasty than most.

But for Real Men, the idea of inventing a cute name for it would be blasphemy. Or treason.

Or, worse, it would be like trying to come up with a different name for the Jeep.

INGREDIENTS
4 slices of bacon
2 quarter-pound hamburger patties – flavoured to taste with Tabasco sauce, plus salt and pepper
2 slices Edam cheese
1 half-inch-thick slice Spanish onion

First, fry the bacon in a skillet until crisp.

Next, remove the bacon from the pan and fry the hamburger patties in the remaining bacon fat.

When the burgers are done on one side, flip them and place a slice of cheese on the cooked side of each burger.

By the time the patty is cooked on the opposite side, the cheese will be melted, and you're ready to construct the finished burger.

Do this:

Place one patty on the bottom half of a hamburger bun, cheese side up.

Place the onion and bacon on top.

Then place the other patty on top of that, cheese side down.

Crown with the top of the bun.

China Syndrome Chilli

A recipe guaranteed to melt down your stomach.

INGREDIENTS
2lbs chuck steak, cut into cubes
1/4 pint vegetable oil
2 onions, chopped
4 cloves garlic, chopped
1 small can of tomato paste
4 tbsp tomato sauce
4 chilli peppers
1 large pinch cayenne pepper
2 tbsp paprika

2 tsp oregano
4 tsp cumin
Salt to taste
1-2 cans red kidney beans

In a large skillet, heat the oil until it's smoking hot. In two batches, brown the beef on all sides and drain the oil from the pan.

Cover the beef with water, cover the skillet and simmer over a low flame for 90 minutes.

(Note: during this entire process, make sure the chilli does not come to a boil, or burn.)

Add onions; simmer for a half-hour, covered.

Following this, add the remaining ingredients and simmer an additional half-hour, uncovered.

Top with red kidney beans.

Yell, 'Come and get it.'

Yield: 4 servings.

Real Men know that Afternoon Delight has nothing at all to do with food.
Quiche Eaters think that it may be some sort of cucumber sandwich.

A Real Man has no idea whatsoever about how to cook an egg plant. And doesn't want to be taught.

Interviews with True Brit Real Cooks (2)

(Note: we talked to Cook Sergeant X somewhere On Active Service Abroad. X is not his
real name. This, along with his number and
location have had to be withheld in the in-
terests of National Security. Luckily his recipe,
previously covered by the Official Secrets Act,
has been given special War Office clearance for
this book.)

Cook Sergeant X, Army Catering Corps, on
secondment to the SAS, looks every inch a
fighting man in his dazzle-camouflaged
kitchen whites. When we talked to him he was
preparing for an air-drop into hostile territory,
where, armed with the menu of the day, he
would be taking orders from the men on the
ground.

   He walked with the carefully stiff-legged
gait of a man with a couple of razor-sharp meat
cleavers strapped to each thigh. On his sleeve
was proudly displayed the Winged Chip Pan
ensignia of his unit together with the motto
Who Flies, Fries.

   His air-portable, all-terrain, field kitchen
pack was being checked over and the instant
heat source module slotted into place. I
noticed the instructions: 'Pull Pin, Take Cover,
Count to Ten and Serve.'

'What're our brave lads having for dinner today, Sgt?'

'Active Service Soup.'

'Soup?'

'Yup. Soup. Comes as a bit of a surprise to a lot of people. They always think the SAS eat raw steak three times a day. But they can't, see. On account of the black balaclavas.'

'Black balaclavas?'

'Yup. You must have seen 'em. The ones they always wear when they're avoiding publicity at press conferences or live on TV Outside Broadcasts. So all you see is a pair of eye-holes in a woolly mask. The thing is these days the lads have to be at instant readiness for an anonymous public appearance anywhere in the world. So they even sleep with them on. And of course it makes for eating difficulties with everything having to be strained through two layers of oiled wool. So it's soup mostly.'

And here is Cook Sergeant X's recipe:

SAS Active Service Soup

To serve a squad of twenty-five men you need:

4oz butter
4 tbsp olive oil
1lb streaky bacon, chopped
4 onions, peeled and chopped
1 head of celery – leaves removed and stalks chopped
    into 1-inch pieces

1lb carrots, peeled and chopped
1lb turnips, peeled and chopped
1 x 15oz tin tomatoes, drained
10 pints stock – Knorr or Oxo cubes will do, but 1
    pint any real ale replacing 1 pint stock and a
    liberal dash of Worcester Sauce will enhance this
    soup
Salt and pepper
2lb leeks, white parts only, peeled and chopped into
    1-inch pieces
1 marrow, hulled and chopped into small chunks
1 tin tomato puree

Melt the butter and oil together in a 24-pint cooking pot with lid. Fry bacon and onions for 5 minutes. Then tip in the celery, carrots, turnips and tinned tomatoes. Cover and sweat for half an hour, stirring occasionally to prevent anything from sticking. Add hot stock and seasoning to taste. Bring to fast boil then turn heat down, cover again and simmer for one hour. Add leeks, marrow and tomato puree. Stir well, cover and simmer again for 40 minutes.

To puree you may push this soup through a sieve, but this is hellish work when dealing with 17 pints of the stuff. A real man knows when to use a very large liquidiser . . . .

Or better still:

Take six prisoners – alive if possible. Grill, trying not to break the skin, and toss heavily into a cell. Leave until well softened-up. Then use them to beat the ingredients into a pulp (or puree, as Quiche Eaters call it). Remember that officers are excluded under the terms of the Geneva Conventions.

Afterwards season to taste. Dispose of the prisoners. For smaller groups, reduce quantities in proportion.

This recipe is also handy for any other group of Real Men who have to remain hooded in the line of duty, such as public executioners and CID officers disguised as Moslem women.

Interviews with True Brit Real Cooks (3)

We were two hundred miles north east of the Shetlands, atop Accidental Petroleum's drilling rig, Red Astaire II. A seventy-kt gale had been blowing from the Arctic for ten days as forty-foot waves crashed against the shuddering structure. On the horizon two supply ships were in difficulties and the Liberian-registered tanker *MV Carefree Navigator* was breaking up as the Officer of the Watch tried to change channels on the radar screen. But after working round the clock in sub-zero temperatures, a hundred and thirty Real Men were in the mood for celebration. Their job was done. Soon the production platforms would be manoeuvred into place and the field come on stream. So it was barbecue time.

Of course True Brit Real Men don't usually eat, let alone cook, in the open air. Only Quiche Eaters build barbecue pits in suburban back gardens and prance around in striped aprons, eyes watering and yelping for the Savlon as they sustain third-degree burns trying to rescue a blackened steaklet that has fallen through the grid into the charcoal. TBRM does not fantasise about Life on the Range, driving twenty thousand head of longhorns down the Chisholm Trail, heading for the Chicago Stockyards. He knows that any cow in this country has just been shipped from intensive rearing unit to supermarket abattoir and that the only Romance in farm life comes in a syringe, courtesy of the Artificial Insemination man.

The only picnic that Real Men has found attractive is that one painted by some Frenchman with naked women sitting around on the grass. And even there Real Man suspects that there were some badly ant-bitten buttocks before the meal was over.

But this time it's a challenge. Way overhead there's a roaring thirty-foot flame as the gas is flared off. The Offshore Cook of the Day, who asked that we do not give his name for fear of reprisals on his family, was being strapped into his steel safety harness, preparatory to being winched up, along with his sack of a hundred and thirty T-bone steaks, by the hovering Offshore Catering Services Wessexburger rescue helicopter. A second helicopter was in readiness in case of an emergency steak ditching.

Soon it would be time for the traditional *Boots Hansen's Platform Blowout*. So, shouting into the gale, we asked him about his special *Force Ten Barbecue Sauce*. Here, as far as we could hear, is the recipe:

This quantity is sufficient to coat 6lbs of good grilling meat.

4 tbsp tomato ketchup
4 tbsp mushroom ketchup
4 tbsp Worcester Sauce

2 tsp sugar
dash red wine vinegar
dash Tabasco sauce
4oz butter, melted

Mix everything together adding a little more melted butter if necessary.

This sauce also makes a tangy accompaniment to another Real North Sea speciality: *Ekofisk Fingers*. These are two feet long and properly should be deep-fried in a light crude oil. Quiche Eaters, unaccustomed to Real Food should be careful. Over-indulgence can lead to Sullum Voe Terminal Indigestion. Such people should stay on shore and be satisfied with a snack at the Refinery.

Real Men do not join food co-operatives in Muswell Hill.

Real Men know that a pulse is a sign of life – not a source of protein.

'Ted can't enjoy a picnic 'til he's secured the perimeter against ants.'

A Bit on the Side with Lunch

Real Men have always had something on the side. Whether it's side arms, side bets, aluminium siding, Valerie Perrine or a sidekick, it's the way Real Men spice up their lives.

The same logic can be applied to a Real Man's meals.

To a Real Man, a hamburger without chips is like Laurel without Hardy.

A ham sandwich without pickles is like Marks without Spencer.

And a meatball hero without chips is like Mobil Oil without a corporate acquisition policy.

This is not to say, however, that just any garnish will do.

Real Men do not put parsley on the side of anything.

They do not augment their sandwiches with orange slices, radish rosettes or cherry tomatoes.

And a Real Man will never eat anything skewered with a frilly toothpick.

When it comes to side dishes, only the following will suffice.

Nat King Cole Slaw

(Prepared to the tune of the 'Christmas Song,' this salad should be eaten while watching *Cat Ballou*.)

INGREDIENTS
1 head of red cabbage, shredded
1 onion, grated
2 green peppers, grated
2 cloves garlic, finely chopped
3 tbsp melted oil
3 tbsp lemon juice
2 tbsp chopped chives
2 tbsp chopped parsley
pinch cayenne pepper, plus salt and pepper to taste

Yield: 6-8 servings

Cabbage shredded on your kitchen counter,
Onions nipping at your nose.

Your grater sounds like an infected choir;
For garlic, please chop up two cloves.

Everybody knows green pepper makes your slaw complete,
While cayenne helps to bring some spice.

Tiny chives, chopped up fine in a bowl;
Add salt and pepper, parsley, till right.

You know the dish is almost done.
Add melted butter, lemons for some fun.

And when you mix it up in a bowl,
You know it's best not to serve too cold.

And so, we're offering this simple dish,
For kids from one to 92.

For though it's been said, many times, many ways,

Happy cole slaw
To you.

Casablanca Baked Beans

Because, 'I'm no good at being noble but it doesn't take much to see that the problems of three little people don't amount to a hill o' beans in this crazy world.'

INGREDIENTS
1½lbs white haricot beans
1½ tsp salt
2 onions, roughly chopped
8 pork spareribs
5 ounces molasses
3 tsp dry mustard
1½ tsp black pepper

Start by soaking the beans in tap water for five hours. Then drain them and place them in a large pot.

In the new pot, cover the beans with fresh water and add salt. Simmer over a low flame for 40 minutes, until the beans are just barely tender. Then drain well. Preheat oven to 250 degrees.

Place the onions and spareribs in a large oven-proof dish. Add the beans and cover the mixture with boiling water. Stir in the molasses; add the mustard and pepper.

Cover and bake for five hours.

NOTE: Check the beans often, adding water as necessary to make sure the mixture is covered.

Yield: 6-8 servings

Real Man Cooking Quiz No 4

Q. How many Quiche Eaters does it take to have a fulfilling sexual experience?

A. Three. Two to do it and one to talk about it on *Claire Rayner's Lifeguide*.

Q. What's the Real Man's idea of group therapy?

A. World War II.

Real Man Cooking Lesson No 4

Three Ways to Call a Real Man to the Dinner Table:

1. 'Grub's up!'
2. 'Soup's on the table.'
3. 'Isn't the *Eurovision Song Contest* about to start on TV?'

Dinner

After a hard day working on the parole board, fighting alligators at Sea World or just destroying people's credit for late payments at the bank, your wife (or girlfriend) deserves a break.

And we're not talking about McDonald's.

As surprising as it may seem, Real Men cook dinner for their loved ones. There are three simple reasons for this:

First, they do it because it helps them avoid doing the dishes.

Second, because there are only so many nights you can eat hamburgers.

And, third, because there's no better setting than champagne and candlelight to coax a girl into bed, or to tell her you're breaking up.

(Admittedly, this may seem a little cynical, but consider this: Where would *you* rather face Barbara Walters? At a 7.30 breakfast in a greasy spoon on Sixth Avenue, a 12.30 lunch in a chichi restaurant where Jacques the maitre d' kisses her hello or a 9.00 tête-à-tête in your apartment?)

Summing up, dinner is the ideal time for romance and seduction.

It's the perfect way to impress a woman – and allows you to show off your collection of 'important 20th-century cultural works,' such as your $300,000 stereo system, clean designer sheets and sixteen-foot Advent television set.

(It's also the perfect time to impress her with your American Express gold card, although this is much more difficult to work into the conversation.)

Needless to say, all of this is irrelevant if Muhammad Ali happens to be making a comeback, live on TV this particular evening.

But if he isn't, sit back, turn down the lights, chill the champagne and slap a Sinatra album on the turntable.

With luck, you'll never get to the food.

Little Caesar Salad

'Now listen up, pal.

'You just can't jump into a steak dinner with some broad and expect things to work out, ya see?

'You gotta ease into things. You gotta take it slow. You gotta work with finesse. And style. Like the way Frank Nitti moved in on Capone's Cicero operations in 1929. Or the way that the Tattaglias muscled in on Vito Corleone in '56.

'So that's why I'm giving you this recipe.

'A lot of people think it's named after some Italian guy, Julius Caesar. But they're wrong, see? He was a pansy. They wrote plays about him. He ran around in a toga. No wonder his friends bumped him off.

'So listen, and listen tight, ya mugs.

I assure you, sir – '82 was an excellent year for ketchup.

'This salad is named after me. It's good. Real good. And nobody crosses Little Caesar:
  'So try it, see?'

CROUTON INGREDIENTS
¼ pint olive oil
3 cloves chopped garlic
8 thick slices crustless white bread

Heat the oil in a skillet until it is smoking hot. Add the garlic, sauté for one minute and then add the bread until golden brown.

SALAD INGREDIENTS
4 heads Webb lettuce
dry mustard, salt and pepper
1 cup grated Parmesan cheese
4 tbsp olive oil
juice of four lemons
4 eggs
8 slices of cooked, crisp bacon
8 chopped anchovy fillets

Tear the lettuce into pieces and place in a very large bowl. Sprinkle with mustard, salt and pepper to taste. Add the Parmesan cheese and toss lightly.

Next, add the lemon juice and oil. Break the eggs onto the lettuce and toss lightly. All the leaves should be coated.

Finally top with crumbled bacon and anchovies. Add croutons, toss well and serve immediately.

Yield: 8 servings

Cream of Beer Soup

By its very nature, soup is not generally considered a Real Man's dish.

It cannot be barbecued. You can't eat it on a bun. It has no bones, cannot be ordered well done, and a steak knife will be useless in its consumption.

Yet, despite this bad news, soup remains an essential ingredient in any romantic dinner.

Thus we offer cream of beer soup.

Admittedly, it's not as Real Man-ish as 'gator bisque. But at least it won't put off women, and surely it's better than starting off your meal with dry-roasted peanuts.

INGREDIENTS
4oz unsalted butter
½ large head of cabbage, shredded fine
1 large onion, chopped fine
1 tbsp flour
1 pint chicken stock
1 pint beer
salt and pepper
¼ pint cream
¼ pint milk

Melt the butter in a 4-quart pot. Add the cabbage and onions and cook them until soft. Then sprinkle the mixture with the flour and cook for one minute longer, stirring constantly.

Add the broth, beer and salt and pepper (to taste), then cover and simmer for one hour.

Ten minutes before the hour is up, heat the milk and cream together in a small pot. The mixture should be hot, but do not let it boil.

Stir the milk and cream into the soup. Serve immediately.

Yield: 5 servings

U.S.D.A. Government Regulation Popovers

If you're going to make a decent popover, you've got to follow the rules. This should be no problem for a Real Man, since he's been playing according to Hoyle, drawing the line, doing it by the book and laying down the law his whole life.

(Yes, we admit it's true that some rules are made to be broken, but not the ones you end up eating.)

The Rules:

1. Milk and eggs must be at room temperature.
2. The eggs must be thoroughly beaten.
3. The muffin tins and oven must be hot.
4. Do not open the oven door while the popovers are cooking.

INGREDIENTS
4 eggs
1lb self-raising flour

1 pint milk
3oz melted butter
½ teaspoon salt
muffin tins
butter to grease the tins

First, place the muffin tins in your oven and preheat to 450 degrees.

Next, beat the eggs in a large bowl, then add the flour, milk, melted butter, and salt, mixing until well blended.

Once the oven and tins are hot, butter the tins and fill each two-thirds of the way up with batter and immediately place each tin in the oven.

Bake at 450 degrees for 20 minutes. Turn the oven down to 350 degrees for another 20 minutes.

Remove and serve.

Yield: 2 dozen

Beef Bourguignon

We admit it.

Bourguignon is a *French* name.

And while we generally have no use for the country that taught the world bad manners and how to surrender, this recipe was simply too delicious to leave out.

So if you're cooking for your buddies, just tell them Beef Bourguignon plays goalie for the Montreal Canadiens – and it's named after his grandfather, who invented the puck.

But if you're cooking for a woman, don't worry.

One taste and she'll think you're James Bond.

INGREDIENTS
12oz bacon
6lbs stewing beef
2 sliced carrots
2 sliced onions
salt and pepper
4 tbsp flour
3 pints red wine
2 tomatoes, chopped
1 large can beef consommé
2 bay leaves
1 tsp thyme
4 cloves of garlic, mashed
cooking oil

Take the bacon, place it in a pot of water and simmer it over a low flame for 10 minutes. Then remove the bacon and cut it into small pieces.

Place three tablespoons of oil in a skillet and sauté the bacon until brown. Remove the bacon, leaving the fat in the skillet.

Next, cut the beef into 2-inch cubes, then brown the cubes on all sides in the oil that remains in the skillet. Add more oil when necessary.

Set the beef aside and brown the carrots and onions in the fat.

Place the bacon, beef and vegetables in a

large casserole; season with salt and pepper to taste. Sprinkle on the flour and toss the ingredients.

Place the casserole in a 400-degree oven until the flour browns. (Toss several times to make sure the flour is cooked; this entire process should take 10 minutes.)

Add the remaining ingredients to the casserole and cover.

Turn the oven down to 325 degrees and cook for three to four hours, or until the beef is fork tender. Remove the beef and boil the liquid away until half is left.

Reheat beef in sauce.

Yield: 4-6 servings

Stuffed Mother-in-Law Chicken

Alas, every once in a while you're forced to break bread with the biggest bread breaker in your life.

This is a dish that will help you survive this ordeal.

It will not only lead your mother-in-law to believe that you actually spend time in the kitchen, but it'll also keep her so busy eating that she won't have time to complain about the money you spent on the 280Z, your excessive drinking habits or the fact that you haven't taken her daughter on a decent vacation in three years.

We'd all like to stuff our mothers-in-law.

This is the only way to do it legally.

STUFFING INGREDIENTS
12 thick slices of crustless day-old bread, cut into
half-inch cubes
4oz parsley, chopped
1 tbsp sage
½ tsp thyme
½ tsp marjoram
½ tsp pepper

Toast the bread cubes in a 275-degree oven until golden brown. Then turn the oven up to 425 degrees. Transfer the bread crumbs to a large bowl and mix in the remaining ingredients. Place aside and prepare the following:

2 large onions, chopped
1 minced chicken liver (from the bird you are
stuffing)
2 sticks celery, chopped
3 tbsp butter

Melt the butter in a pan and sauté these ingredients for ten minutes over a medium flame. Then scrape into the stuffing mixture and beat well.

1 egg, beaten lightly
¼ pint chicken stock
2 tbsp cream

Add these liquids to the stuffing mixture, beat until well blended and stuff into a four-pound raw roasting chicken.

Next, truss the bird. (No, this does not

Ok – I can't take any more. Here's Don Corleone's recipe for linguini with red clam sauce.

mean ordering some therapeutic device for it from the back of *Popular Science*. The process is also known as sealing the bird – which you can accomplish by placing aluminium foil over the open cavity and tying the legs together.)

Place the chicken in a roasting pan. Smear the chicken all over with soft butter, sprinkle it with salt and pepper – and place it on the middle shelf of a preheated 425-degree oven.

Brown the chicken for 15 minutes. Turn the oven down to 350 degrees and cook for about 90 minutes. Baste occasionally with its own juices.

To see if the chicken is done, pierce the leg joint with a fork; the juice should run clear yellow.

Yield: 4 servings

Infidelity Fricassee

Your girlfriend has just caught you in bed with her college room-mate.

No matter how you slice it, your goose is cooked. You're in a jam. You're in a pickle. You're in hot water. You've gotten yourself into some fine kettle of fish – and the icing on the cake is that your girlfriend is stewing.

No, this is not the time to talk turkey.

It's the time to act like a chicken, and cook one.

Admittedly, this may seem like a half-baked idea at first.

But it's a fast way to dilute the problem

before she boils over, scrambles your brains
and ices the relationship.

Of course, if she fails, you might try
another tack:

Tell her that if she can't stand the heat, she
should get out of the bedroom.

INGREDIENTS
2lbs chicken breasts halved (bone in)
½ tsp salt
½ tsp pepper
8oz flour
1 tbsp butter
3 tbsp cooking oil
1 onion, chopped
1 can cream of chicken soup
1 potato, diced
1 carrot, diced
½ lb fresh mushrooms, sliced
pinch of basil
1 bay leaf
4oz of cream

Preheat oven to 350 degrees. Place the salt,
pepper and flour in a large grocery bag and
shake to mix the ingredients. Add the chicken
breasts, and shake again until they're completely coated.

Over a medium flame, heat the butter and
oil in a casserole dish, add the chicken and
onion. Sauté until brown.

Add enough chicken broth to cover the
meat, then add the basil and bay leaf. Cover
and place in oven for 30 minutes.

After 30 minutes, add the carrot, potato and mushrooms to the dish and cook for an additional 30 minutes.

Uncover your casserole, pour in the cream, stir, serve and pray she forgives you.

Yield: 4 servings

An Important Note on Steak

In America today, there are at least 30,000 different steak recipes.

All of them are good.

Steak, you see, is the Real Man's birthday cake; and while we prefer a plain, simple sirloin, fried in a pan with a touch of butter and oil, we would not be so presumptuous as to force our will on you.

The way we see it, telling a Real Man how to prepare his steak would be like telling him how to ride his horse, drive his car or make love to his girlfriend.

And among Real Men this just isn't done.

How do you want your steak? Rare or on the hoof?

Adam's Spare Ribs

The original Real Man recipe.

INGREDIENTS
4lbs fresh pork spare ribs
½ can canned beef consommé
½ pint tomato sauce
½ pint red wine
½ pint orange juice
4 cloves of garlic, sliced
1 tsp oregano
1 tsp basil
4 tsp salt
⅔ cup olive oil

In a large roasting pan, mix all ingredients except the meat. Then add the ribs to the pan and marinade them in your refrigerator for a minimum of 24 hours.

There are two options for final preparation:

You can either bake the ribs in a 350-degree oven for 45 minutes, or just grill them on your barbecue. Either way, make sure you baste them during cooking with the marinade.

NOTE: for an additional treat, try smothering the cooked ribs with the Georgia peach sauce described on page 54.

Yield: 2 servings

Ten-Penny Nail Baked Potato

Real Men nail down multibillion-dollar defence contracts.

They nail the opposing quarterback.

They nail Britt Ekland.

After which, a Real Man celebrates with steak and a baked potato.

The following recipe will facilitate the cooking of the baked potato, insuring that it cooks evenly and quickly, without the outer portion drying.

After all, it's the Real Man who should be hard as nails, not his baked potato.

INGREDIENTS
baking potatoes
ten-penny nails
a hammer

Scrub your spuds and drain them.

One at a time, stand the potatoes up on end and drive a nail through the centre, lengthwise.

Bake in a 375-degree oven until soft when pierced with a fork.

Add sour cream, chives, crumbled bacon, shredded cheese or sautéed garlic with melted butter to taste.

TECHNICAL NOTE: According to Mister Wizard, the nail acts as a heat conductor. He also advises that you remove it before eating.

Seafood

Real Men love the sea.

Without the world's oceans, there would be no atomic submarines, aircraft carriers, battle-ships or amphibious troop carriers. And Jacques Cousteau would be a coal miner.

Real Men are also fond of lakes and rivers, because they can dredge them, dam them, shoot their rapids and cross them with suspension bridges. They also provide excellent places for hiding cars, old tyres and friends who've fallen from favour.

Despite this love of aquatic acreage, however, Real Men are not particularly fond of aquatic life.

If cattle had fins, Real Men would eat more seafood.

Real Men do not eat weakfish. They don't carp on anything, flounder, clam up or cut bait. A Real Man would never eat anything called 'shrimp'; he thinks tuna are better left to Russian trawlers; and let's not discuss what he thinks of crabs.

Going still further, Real Men admire barra-cuda, sharks, swordfish and marlin – and as such could never eat them.

Real Men think goldfish make nice house plants; they admire the name mussel, and while most Real Men view their lives as a continual struggle to swim upstream, they do not eat salmon.

Real Men *do* have one puzzling question about seafood, however.

Most seafood companies advertise fish that 'doesn't have that fishy taste.'

To this, Real Men wonder:

'If you don't want food that tastes fishy, why eat fish?'

True Brit Real Men and Fish

TBRM eat a restricted range of fish dishes.
For instance:

Cod-and-chips
Cod-and chips-twice
Cod-and-double-chips
Rock-and-chips
Haddock-and-chips
Saveloys
Plaice-and-chips
Fishcakes
and
Krayfish Pie (take half a shark and a dozen piranhas . . . .)

Interviews with True Brit Real Cooks (4)

We talked to RFU-approved cook Chip O'Larta at the annual end-of-season dinner and demolition derby of the Northern Luddites Rugby Club. The Luddites are a touring side. Their coach and keeper explained the club philosophy to me: 'Whereas sides like the Barbarians are traditionally dedicated to open Rugby, all brilliant inventive back play and attacking-from-your-own-goal-line stuff – Quiche-rugger we call it – the Luddites play Real Rugby. Gruelling, grudging, mud-and-sweat forward struggles. Each member of the touring party is carefully picked on his record of mayhem and gratuitous destruction over the season.

A typical Luddite is sixteen stone of malevolent thug. A typical Luddite movement takes place deep in the heart of a collapsed scrum and involves twisting an opponent's testicles off. You can always tell that the Luddites have been playing by the state of the pitch afterwards. Acres of untouched green grass and what looks like a bomb crater in the middle where they have rucked, mauled and hacked away for eighty minutes.

Quiche-eating stand-off halves may get praised for their incisive Rugby brains. Luddites know that the game is played not with the brain but with the head. And the boot, the fist and the knee. Indeed many Luddites are entirely unaware that the game involves the use of a ball and can be quite dumbfounded if they come upon one at the bottom of a ruck.

One obvious characteristic of a Luddite player is his vast pendant paunch. Indeed when packing low in the scrum their bellies trail on the ground like a herd of prime Friesians before milking-time. Since a Luddite never actually has to run but must avoid getting knocked over, it is important that they are ballasted down not just with beer but with Real Food.'

As we talked to Chip the Chef in his kitchen, we could hear through the swinging doors a bellowing bedlam of song and retching, mingling with the crash of broken glass. Thirty Luddites were waiting for dinner. There was a momentary hush as they bowed their heads in remembrance of twelve team members who were absent, in hospital. We quickly took advantage of the lull to ask Chip what he would be serving.

'Bread rolls to start with. Large baskets of bread rolls. That keeps 'em occupied for some time. We get them specially ordered in. Your Rugby club dinner's bread roll is pretty special. It has to be aerodynamically sound and have a very hard crust. After all there's no point in throwing a soft roll when the object of the exercise is to stun the man at the far end of the table.

After that we put the emphasis on soft food. Very few of the lads have their own teeth any more and by half way through the meal most of them will have accidentally coughed their dentures out into the urinal. So it's well-cooked braising steak with mashed potatoes and carrots. For pudding it's apple pie and mock cream. They love the mock cream and play in it for hours. At Christmas of course we serve the traditional Christmas scrum pudding, liberally doused with flaming after-shave.'

So for anyone who has to cater for a team dinner, or even one player, here is Chip's recipe for *Garryowen Goulash*.

Feeds six rugger players. You need:

Beef dripping
3lb quality chuck steak, cut into large chunks
3 tbsp flour
6 medium onions, chopped
2 cloves garlic, crushed
1 pint Guinness or decent real ale
salt and pepper
1 bay leaf
1 tsp thyme

Heat oven to 325 degrees. Melt a little beef dripping in a large frying pan. Roll steak chunks in the flour to coat thoroughly and brown them in batches, removing each batch to a fireproof casserole. Add more dripping if necessary. Then tip all the onions and garlic into the pan and fry gently for 5 minutes. Add to meat. Discard frying pan and set casserole onto flame. Add beer, seasoning, bay leaf and thyme. Bring to boil and check flavour. Then

94

cover and transfer to oven. Cook for 2½-3
hours. This casserole is well-behaved and will
stand any amount of cooking – a lower temperature for 5 hours will do no harm.

Eat with creamy mashed potatoes. You
may also offer bowls of green salad tossed in a
hearty vinaigrette, but it is unlikely that this
will be appreciated. At least as food. It is more
than likely that the salad will indeed be tossed
and the empty bowls used for quite other
purposes.

Serve with a quick two-handed put-in between the opposing front rows and retreat
hastily to the base of the scrum.

Interviews with True Brit Real Cooks (5)

We were over five hundred feet up on the moors behind Clitheroe. Ahead the dark looming bulk of Pendle Hill was hunched against a rain-filled sky. In this strange part of the world where folk-memories of the Lancashire Witches are still alive, a man can still stumble across vestiges of near-forgotten craft skills and traces of an older way of life.

We had been sent to this bleak place by an aged Burnley informant. It was to prove the last stage of a bizarre and sometimes wearisome quest. Here, it had been hinted, we might find the last of the old Wesselmen.

Once the plains of the Ribble Valley had been thick with them and their produce known and eaten as far south as Macclesfield, but the inexorable advance of Fast Food and supermarket standardisation had driven them out of business and into the hills where they had clung on grimly, purveyors of a vanishing culinary art.

These can be dangerous parts for a stranger and, acting on the advice of a helpful pensioner we had found in a pub in Oldham at closing time, we travelled disguised as traditional Lancashire mill girls. Pulling our loosely knitted shawls about us in the raw fell wind, our clogs slipping on the worn cobblestones, we staggered up the one-in-four and out on to the open moors. Sheep's skulls grinned up at us from the heather as we skirted carefully round the edge of a tripe dump. Smears of jellied cow heel and discarded potted meat dishes led us ever onward. Borne up from below came snatches of brass band music and the smell of a thousand Chinese take-aways.

A thin, chill rain began to fall and we were often tempted to turn back. Even Real Men cannot stand too much Reality. But we knew that we were on the track of a True Brit eating experience that is fast disappearing – indeed believed by many to be already extinct.

And so we found him: the Last Wesselman. His stone-built cottage seemed to grow out of the very rock. He saw us and knew, as if by instinct, what we sought. Beckoning, he led us to a low outhouse and, peering in, we saw, dangling in rows from the smoke-blackened rafters, the raw materials of his gristly trade. This was what we had hoped against hope to find. *Wessel in the making.

So what is Wessel, many a Real Man will be asking? A fabled Lancashire delicacy, it is made out of cooked bulls' penis. Three feet of solid protein, in years gone by it nourished and sustained many a working man. It was the centrepiece of many a Wakes Week feast. Cured, smoked or kippered, a Wesselbutty made a tasty midday snack. Even today the song *Wessel While You Work* can be heard,

*Or Wizzle, Wezzel etc. Like many gems of oral culture, the spelling has never been standardised.

accompanied by a curious skipping game, in many a children's playground. And it has been known in other countries and cultures as well. BAOR readers may well have come across the *Horse Wessel Song* in Germany. The well-known couplet in *Omar Khayyam*

> And He that with his Hand the
> Wessel made
> Will surely not in after Wrath destroy

suggests that it was eaten in ancient Persia.

Now, alas, Wessel has gone the way of the steam engine and the cotton industry. We were indeed lucky to track down this morsel from all our yesterdays.

Over a steaming bowl of oatmeal and freshly mashed Wessel, we tried to cut short an endless flow of reminiscence. He talked of true Wessel, taken from a mature bull, and Poorman's or bullock's Wessel. He talked of canalside pubs where the old Navigators – the original Navvies – competed in drinking a Yard of Ale and eating a Yard of Wessel.

The shades of night were falling fast as, by the flickering, fitful light of a dripping and string lamp, we took down this finest of all Wessel recipes.

Wessel Wellington

18" bull's penis, appropriately trimmed
12oz self raising flour
4oz white breadcrumbs
1lb fresh beef suet
large pinch salt
cold water (approx 8 tbsp)
4oz butter
1lb flat black mushrooms, chopped
1lb onions, chopped
seasoning

Preheat oven to 375 degrees. Prepare the suet pastry. In a large bowl mix together the flour, salt, breadcrumbs and suet. Add sufficient cold water to form a stiff dough. Divide in two and set aside in a cool place to rest.

Gently fry the onions in the butter for 5 minutes. Add the mushrooms and continue cooking for a further 5 minutes. Set aside.

Take the pastry and roll out each half to form rectangles 20" x 8". On one sheet place half the stuffing mixture, spreading it flat to within 1" of the edges. Lay the bulls penis onto this and cover with remainder of the stuffing. Place the second sheet of pastry on top and bring all the edges together to form a long roll. Seal edges firmly with water. Any trimmings may be used to decorate the top. Remember to pierce the pastry once or twice to allow steam to escape. Now for the tricky part: hold one end of the pastry and gently coil it around itself to resemble an ammonite or a Danish pastry. Place coil onto a baking tray and brush liberally with egg and milk. Place in oven covered loosely with a double layer of greased foil for 1 hour. Then uncover and allow to cook for one more hour or until nicely browned.

Serve with well-boiled savoy cabbage and roasted turnips.

Other True Brit Real regional dishes:

CID Grilled Suspect

UDR Steak Out
(to cook, detonate with a controlled explosion . . . .)

Enriched Uranium Melt-Down, Sizewell-style
(cook in a Pressurised Water Reactor . . . .)

Only Real Rastas eat curried goat, rice and peas.

Afters

A Real Man finishes what he begins.

He does not give up in the middle of a job. He does not end things in a half-assed manner. He does not get substituted, retire hurt or refuse at the last fence.

This same rigorous moral code can be applied to the process of finishing a dinner.

Where lesser men try to pick at the pudding before the meal, a Real Man is content to wait.

Where lesser men might serve shop-bought cake or ice cream, a Real Man goes the distance and creates his own.

Real Men understand that sooner or later we all get our just desserts.

And he's willing to wait, not just because it tastes better at the end of the meal – but because he realises he needs the extra sugar to face the rest of the evening's challenges.

Smuggler's Pecan Rum Pie

You can always buy the rum for this dessert in your local liquor store; but buying it from a smuggler makes a far better story over coffee.

INGREDIENTS FOR TWO PIES
½lb sugar
¼lb butter, melted

4 eggs, lightly beaten
6oz flour
6 tbsp dark rum
1 tsp salt
2 tsp almond extract
2 tsp vanilla
15fl oz golden syrup

Preheat oven to 250 degrees. Beat together in a large mixing bowl, then add:

1½lb chopped pecans – (unsalted peanuts will do for the poorer Real Man)

Beat well again.

Pour the mixture into two unbaked 9-inch pie shells. (You can cheat and purchase them in the frozen-food section of your super-market.)

Bake in a 350-degree oven for 30 to 45 minutes, or until the filling has set.

Serve hot.

Great Moments in Real Man Cuisine

The setting is Havana. 1959. New Year's Eve
The Godfather, part II:
When asked if he'd like a banana daiquiri, Al Pacino replies:
'No.'

Rum Cake

At last: a new way of consuming rum.

INGREDIENTS
4oz unsalted butter, at room temp
8oz sugar
3 eggs
½ tsp baking powder
1lb flour
6 tbsp Dark Navy Rum
12oz currants, or raisins
½lb chopped walnuts

Preheat oven to 350 degrees. In a large bowl, beat the sugar into the softened butter until fluffy and white. Beat eggs in well.

Now, in a separate bowl, combine the baking powder and flour.

Beat the rum into the eggs and butter, then add the flour mixture, fruit and nuts, mixing well.

Take a loaf pan, smear it with butter and dust it with flour. Pour in the batter and bake for about one and three-quarter hours, or until a knife plunged in the centre of the cake comes out dry.

Yield: 1 9x5x3 inch cake.

Beer Sherbet

Admittedly, Real Men love Baskin-Robbins' 'rocky road,' 'German chocolate cake' and 'pralines & cream.'

But the company does have one shortcoming: no liquor licence.

INGREDIENTS FOR ONE QUART
½ lb sugar
10fl oz water
juice from half an orange
juice from half a lemon
1½ pints beer
1 egg white
5 lb crushed ice
1 lb coarse salt

In a large saucepan, bring the water and sugar to a boil, until the bubbles appearing on the surface are thick. Let cool – then mix in the beer and fruit juices.

In a separate bowl, beat the egg white until stiff. Fold the egg white into the syrup mixture. Pour this into a three-quart saucepan.

Place the ice and salt in a stopped-up sink. Nest the saucepan in the ice and beat the mixture until the sherbet is thick.

Freeze overnight.

Sweets

One issue needs to be settled. Real Men are not afraid to eat sweet things. They are prepared to stand out against the tide of propaganda about tooth decay, gum rot, plaque and general dental hygiene that comes at us from all sides these days.

Real Men consider that if the miracle products of the toothpaste industry were all they're cracked up to be, and if the years of intensive scientific training given to the country's dentists had any effect, then between them they'd be able to cope with any minor damaging side-effects caused by eating sweets, biscuits and cake.

After all, who'd buy central heating from a company that suggested that after installation, you should buy six layers of thermal underwear and be prepared to shiver from September to May. Or put your car in for patent rustproofing treatment by a firm who advised you not to take it out in the rain for ever afterwards.

So why be swayed by toothpaste men and dentists. Either their treatments work and are worth paying for, or they don't and aren't. Thus it is that a Real Man eats what he wants and at intervals goes along to the dentist, points at his row of blackened stumps and says: 'Fix this. And no moral lectures.'

So here's a wonderfully sweet recipe for

Chocolate Brownies. Eat them and wave two fingers at the Man with the High Speed Drill. And remember, a redundant toothbrush is a handy spark plug cleaner.

Chocolate Brownies

2oz cocoa plus 5 tbsp water
4oz unsalted butter
2 eggs
8oz caster sugar
3oz plain flour
½ tsp baking powder
pinch salt
4oz walnut pieces

8" square cake tin, greased and lined

Preheat oven to 350 degrees. Mix cocoa and water to a cream in a medium sized saucepan. Add melted butter and warm gently but do not allow to boil. Sift flour, sugar, salt and baking powder together and stir into cocoa mixture. Lastly add walnuts.

Place mixture in tin and bake for 35 minutes until a brown crust has formed. Allow to cool slightly, then cut into squares. Store in an airtight tin.

Quiche – The Final Frontier

And to end with, any True Brit Real Man knows deep down inside that the awful day may come when he will have to tread boldly into something nasty, step where no Real Man should go. He may not only have to eat but actually *cook* Quiche.

Imagine. It is late Saturday afternoon. You and a couple of Real Accomplices have tunnelled your way into the basement of your local macrobiotic health food store. Because Real Men know that health food stores make Real Money. Months of careful planning are about to pay off. Swiss banking law and extradition treaties have been researched. Information has been painstakingly collected and the intricate security system subverted. The week's takings are in the safe. This is the Big One.

Now the whole weekend lies ahead but you will need every minute of it as you work with silent intensity to cut your way into the massive strong room and clear it out.

And there is one problem. Food. There can be no sending out for fish and chips while you work, yet the three of you must eat in order to keep your strength up for the long hours of endeavour. However the raw ingredients of a thousand meals lie all about you in the shop. There is no alternative. You will have to choke back your revulsion and cook Quiche.

Take heart. It will not be pleasant but the

memory will fade as you count the money later. First, a word about the ingredients, health food style:

Eggs. Be warned. Health food, free range eggs are not easily recognised. Their most obvious characteristic is that they are three times the price of proper eggs. So look about you and you should see a pile of what appear to be elliptical snooker balls covered with feathers and chicken droppings. You will obviously wish to avoid handling these revolting objects yourself and there is a strong case for taking a hostage. Then persuade him, by means of certain observations about the future well-being of his family, to clean them.

Spring onions. Any vegetables you see will be what is called *organically grown*. Again the most obvious characteristic of these stone-age fore-runners of normal veg is price. They are also covered with mud and well-rotted manure. Any green leaves, the things having been grown without benefit of Fisons or ICI, will already be largely eaten by insects. Do not be surprised to find them crawling with wildlife. Using your *Collins Field Guide to All that is Loathsome in Nature*, you should be able to identify several species. Look particularly for the slug. These come in several shades of black/grey/brown and are called slugs because they are sluggish. Their immobility and general lack of liveliness is probably caused by their vegetarian diet. You should also be able to spot several varieties of caterpillar. Note especially the Brown Tail Moth caterpillar. This is hairy and poisonous. Earthworms and a wide range of revolting grubs will be wrapped round any root crops. Apart from this, natural organic veg are small, stringy and misshapen.

Flour. This will be marked '100% Wholemeal Flour' and, unnervingly, will be brown. The packet will be covered with small print that goes on about enzymes, vitamins, bran and wheatgerm. Do not read all this. It will only put you off.

Fat. This will have to be either sunflower oil or low-cholesterol, high-in-polyunsaturates, 100%-guaranteed-pure-vegetable-matter, tested-without-cruelty-to-animals, margarine. By now you will have realised that all health food packets are literally smothered in long words. This accounts for the fact that dyslexic or ESN health food addicts, particularly of the macrobiotic tendency, usually die of starvation whilst trying to read the labels.

Salt. Even salt in these benighted places is odd. It will be called something like Pure Sea Salt and comes in rock-hard lumps that have to be ground up before it is of any use. Again this is a job for a hostage. Get him to stamp up and down on it while you stand by with a whip for when he flags.

Sugar. Look for Raw Cane Sugar. This is dark brown, sticky and tastes funny. Do not use in tea.

Cheese. Don't bother to look for sensible pre-sliced, packaged cheese. Here it will be rennet-free goats milk cheese and appear as a smelly whitish runny mess in a bag.

Cream. Probably made from soya milk or cashews.

By now you will have realised that the preparation of Quiche-style meals takes hours. Luckily you have the weekend ahead of you. Just be thankful that the recipe does not call for beans since these do not come ready-to-eat in tins but have to be soaked in cold water for about the length of time it takes Liverpool to wrap-up the League Championship in an average season.

Meat. There isn't any, not even bacon. These places don't go in for it. This is just as well. Any health food meat would have to come from a free-range animal that had died of natural causes – i.e. either old age or some vile wasting disease, covered in parasites. So you're well out of that one.

GBH Quiche

THE PASTRY
½lb flour
7oz fat
salt
1 tbsp sugar

Mix together the flour, sugar and a pinch of salt. Work in the fat until the mixture reminds you of coarse sand. Roll into a ball, wrap it up and leave it alone for an hour or so.

The pastry will be too crumbly to roll out so you will have to press it into the quiche dish with your fingers until it is of an even thickness. Remember whatever you do not to leave any prints in it.

Prick the bottom with a fork or it will swell up like a balloon as you bake it for 10 minutes at 450 degrees.

In the circumstances outlined here, you may have to use, instead of an oven, an empty safe, pre-heated with a thermic lance or blow torch.

THE QUICHE MIXTURE
1 bunch chopped spring onions
fat
6-8oz cheese
3 eggs, well beaten
½ pint of nearest thing to cream you can find in the place
salt and pepper

Saute the onions in 1 tablespoon of fat and line the bottom of the pastry crust. On top, spread the cheese, cut up into small lumps. Mix the eggs in with the 'cream', adding salt and pepper. Pour this lot over the cheese and bake for 15 minutes at 450 degrees. Then turn down the heat to 350 degrees and bake for another 15 minutes or so.

You can eat it either hot or cold. This amount will serve 6 – or 3 if you're all sufficiently hungry to forget what it is you're eating.

One helpful side-effect is that afterwards the police will think they're on the track of a vegetarian gang and will spend their time watching Holland & Barrett shops and harassing people carrying copies of *Here's Health* or Barbara Cartland romantic novels.

Whilst you of course will be on a Brazilian beach, tucking into 2lb prime fillet steaks.

The Final Advantage to Cooking Your Own Meals

It's midnight. You and Jacqueline Bisset have just finished dinner in the most elegant part of your apartment.

The beef bourguignon was perfect. The popovers, sublime. You've displayed the table manners of Fred Astaire, using every knife, fork and spoon correctly – and not once did you get up to check the score of the Raiders game.

As you take your final sip of champagne, it's the most anxious moment of the evening.

The candles are low. The music, romantic. You look softly into her light-blue eyes; she smiles and purses her lips invitingly over the champagne glass she's brought to her mouth.

It's time for your big move.

Slowly, you reach across the table and squeeze her hand; it feels like the inside of a rose petal. You dream of satin sheets, limousine rides at dawn, and a passionate embrace at dusk on the beach at St. Martin. As your lips brush across her cheek you gently coo in her ear:

'It's your turn to take out the garbage.'

Real Men, you see, understand there is no such thing as a free lunch.

Or, for that matter, a free dinner.